This Journal Belongs to

Published by

Real Joy Publications

Made in the USA
Las Vegas, NV
25 April 2025

21365352R00066